'If only they could talk!'

ANIMAL MAGIC

Mike Hollist's
amazing animal photos

Words by Shaun Usher

The publishers wish to thank Mike Hollist for his magnificent
photographs, Shaun Usher for his witty aphorisms, and the
Daily Mail for making it all possible.

Published in Great Britain in 1988 by
Exley Publications Ltd,
16 Chalk Hill, Watford, Herts WD1 4BN, United Kingdom.

Second printing 1988
Third printing 1989
Fourth and fifth printings 1990

British Library Cataloguing in Publication Data
    Hollist, Mike
    Animal magic
    1. Animals. Illustrations
    I. Title   II. Usher, Shaun
    591'022'2

ISBN 1-85015-118-0 (h/b)

Typeset by Brush Off Studios, St Albans, Herts.
Printed and bound in Hungary.

"I can save the front ones, but that molar's got to come out."

"Nice daffodil, but it needs more mayonnaise."

"I never need hairspray on <u>mine</u>, David."

"Who's a pretty boy then?"

"<u>Told</u> you I'm a boy!"

In camera

"Sure you shaved this morning, soldier?"

"Take notes, class – we'll be asking questions later."

"Take me with you, you <u>promised</u> ..."

Hindsight

"My dear, <u>everyone's</u> wearing them this year ..."

"How much is that human in the window?"

"Like all my kittens, they're going through an awkward stage."

That tickles!

" 'With one bound, Rover was free and ---' Turn the page, dummy!"

Sealed with a kiss.

"Blow in their ear, works every time ..."

Policeman's lot

"Their legs may be longer but I can't help thinking mine have a certain elegance ..."

"Now you know my folks – Harry, Barry, Larry and Gary,

Shari, Carrie, Mary, Murray, Maurie ..."

A stable, affectionate relationship.

"Shove off, Bambi, or I'll get my brother onto you."

"I know I left it in here somewhere."

"All together lads, 'Forty fahsand fevvers on a Frush,' in C ..."

"On behalf of my fellow candidates ..."

"Kiss me goodnight, Sergeant Major!"

"Tell me a story …"

"It's an amusing little water, a bit brash, obviously from the
southern slopes, of course it was a good year,
not a great year but ..."

*"I never bite people, but if you're the weather forecaster,
I just might make an exception ..."*

"Who loves ya, baby?"

"I do!"

Togetherness

"*My private term for this activity is 'Jump-a-Yuppie'.*"

"Who needs a sturdy branch – what are friends for!"

"As I told the Party in '63 ..."

"You are getting sleepy, very sleepy ..."

Tiger by the tail, heart in mouth.

"Once upon a time ..."

"You cannot be serious!"

"My front's my best side."

"I distinctly ordered a <u>tooth</u>brush!"

Go faster, Stripes!

"Any day now, not that it's your business."

"Good question …"

Lip service

"You scratch my back ..."

Attraction of opposites

"Close my eyes and wish – feathers for ol' Four-legs there and a deep, melodious bark for me."

"Funny lot, humans – they make these noises in daylight, too ..."

Double act.

"Right, little buddy, which <u>did</u> come first – you or the egg?"

"Between ourselves, vegetarian diets are <u>boring</u>."

"I'll never touch the hard stuff again."

"Call me old fashioned, but I'm sure that stuff's bad for you."

"He kidded me this was a designer nosebag ..."

"Where's the zipper?"

"Bring on the Mad Hatter!"

"*Add some daisies and the merest scrap of veil, and you've got a sale.*"

"Top of the world, Ma!"

"She'll never stare <u>me</u> out!"

"Five and five is, um ... plus <u>his</u> five makes, er ..."

"That's all, folks!"